GNARLY

SPORTS INJURIES

JOHN PERRITANO

red rhino b**OO**k s®

NONFICTION

Photo credits: page 14: Cal Sport Media / Alamy.com; page 16: Rena Schild / Shutterstock.com; page 28: B.Stefanov / Shutterstock.com ;page 29: B.Stefanov / Shutterstock.com; page 34: Ivica Drusany / Shutterstock.com; page 39: Scott Prokop / Shutterstock.com; page 41: lev radin / Shutterstock.com; page 44: rook76 / Shutterstock.com; page 44: Olga Popova / Shutterstock.com page 45: Elena Korchenko / Alamy.com; All other source images from Shutterstock.com

SADDLEBACK
EDUCATIONAL PUBLISHING
www.sdlback.com

ISBN-13: 978-1-68021-071-2
ISBN-10: 1-68021-071-8
eBook: 978-1-63078-381-5

Printed in Malaysia

22 21 20 19 18   2 3 4 5 6

TRANER MIDDLE SCHOOL
1700 CARVILLE DR.
RENO, NV 89512

TABLE OF CONTENTS

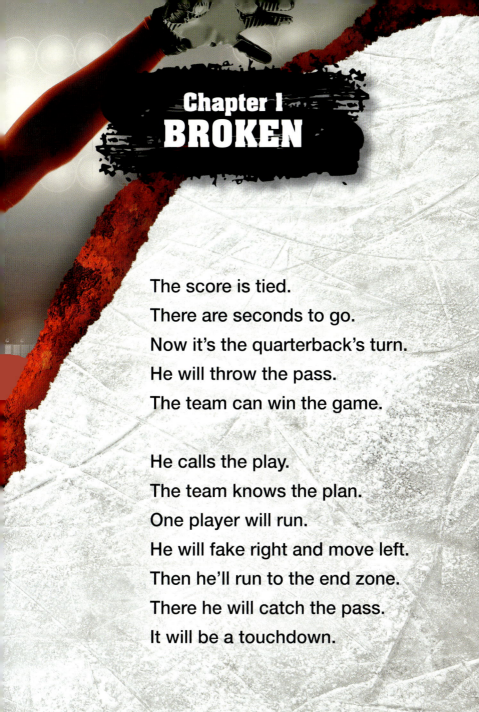

Chapter 1
BROKEN

The score is tied.

There are seconds to go.

Now it's the quarterback's turn.

He will throw the pass.

The team can win the game.

He calls the play.

The team knows the plan.

One player will run.

He will fake right and move left.

Then he'll run to the end zone.

There he will catch the pass.

It will be a touchdown.

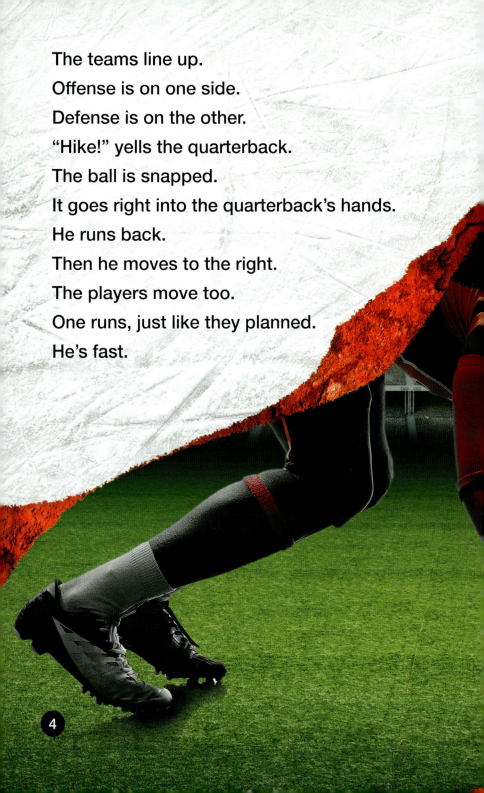

The teams line up.

Offense is on one side.

Defense is on the other.

"Hike!" yells the quarterback.

The ball is snapped.

It goes right into the quarterback's hands.

He runs back.

Then he moves to the right.

The players move too.

One runs, just like they planned.

He's fast.

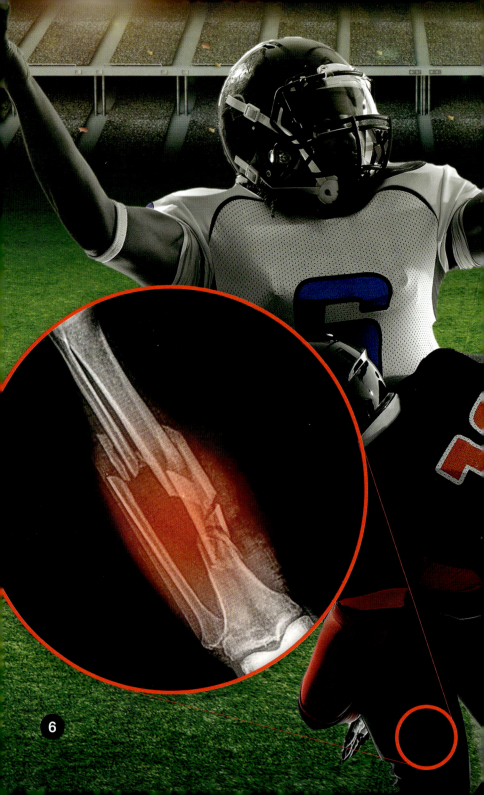

A linebacker from the other team moves too.

He's 280 pounds of pure muscle.

The big man runs for the quarterback.

Crash!

The quarterback cries out.

He falls to the ground.

His leg is hurt.

It's bad.

The play is over.

The leg is broken.

Bone pokes through skin.

Blood pours out.

It's ugly.

He may never play again.

Players get hurt in sports.

Some *injuries* are small.

There are bloody noses.

Some get black eyes.

Fingers break.

Other injuries are *gnarly*.

Bones rip skin.

Eyes pop out.

Ears hang off.

It's a risk athletes take.

People have always loved sports.
Some want to play.
Others like to watch.

The Greeks started the Olympics.
It was almost 3,000 years ago.
Men boxed.
Some ran foot races.
Others raced horses.

Many got hurt.

People wrote about it.

One of those people was Homer.

He was a poet and sports writer.

Homer wrote about a boxing match.

Two fighters punched each other.

Pow!

One man got hit in the jaw.

It was a hard hit.

Friends ran to him.

They pulled him away.

Homer saw it all.

The man's head hung limp.

He was spitting blood.

The Mayans lived 4,000 years ago.

They were in Mexico and Central America.

Sports were big.

One game was rough.

It was called the ball game.

The game was played on a long court.

It was shaped like a rectangle.

The court had walls with hoops.

The hoops were made of stone.

Teams raced up and down the court.

They chased a heavy ball.

The goal was to score.

Players shot the ball through a hoop.

Then they got a point.

Players could not use their hands.

Any other body part was okay.

Feet, legs, shoulders, and elbows were fair game.

It was brutal.

Many got hurt.

Noses gushed blood.

Bones broke.

Heads cracked open.

The winners became rich.

The losers were killed.

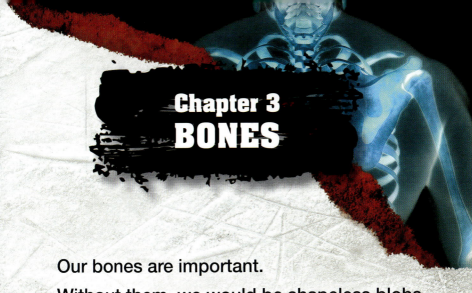

Chapter 3
BONES

Our bones are important.

Without them, we would be shapeless blobs.

Our skeletons hold us up.

They protect our insides.

Vitamins are stored in our bones.

Minerals are too.

Adult human skeletons have 206 bones.

Babies start with 270.

Many fuse together.

That is why adults have fewer bones.

Some bones are big.

Others are tiny.

They connect at *joints*.

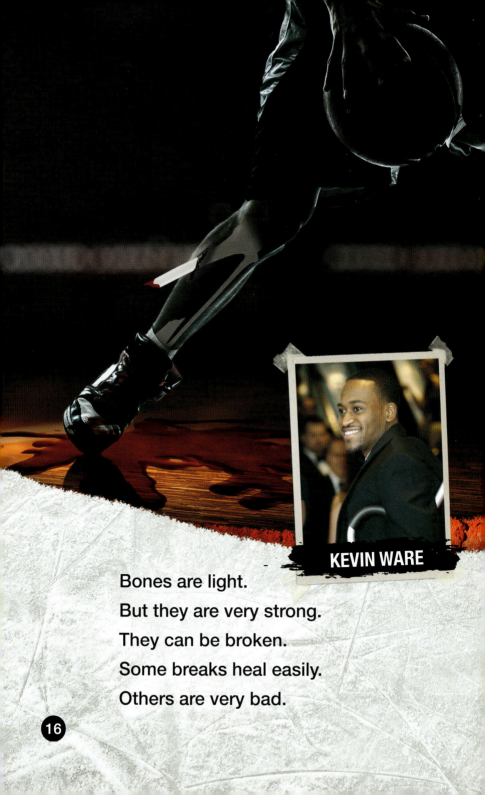

KEVIN WARE

Bones are light.
But they are very strong.
They can be broken.
Some breaks heal easily.
Others are very bad.

16

It was 2013.
Kevin Ware was a basketball player.
He tried to block a ball.
His jump went wrong.
Snap!

His right leg broke.
The shin bone snapped.
It popped out through his skin.
Blood gushed.
Everyone saw it.
Many looked away.
Some cried.

WEIRD SPORTS INJURIES

LIONEL SIMMONS

SPORT: Basketball
INJURY: Wrist
HOW: Played too many video games

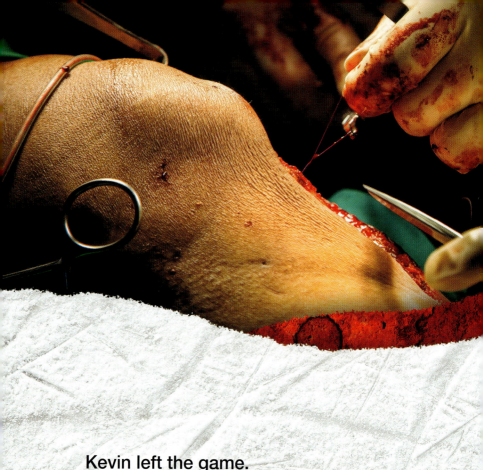

Kevin left the game.

He went to the hospital.

Doctors screwed his bones together.

They used a metal rod.

The rod held the bones in place.

His skin was sewn back together.

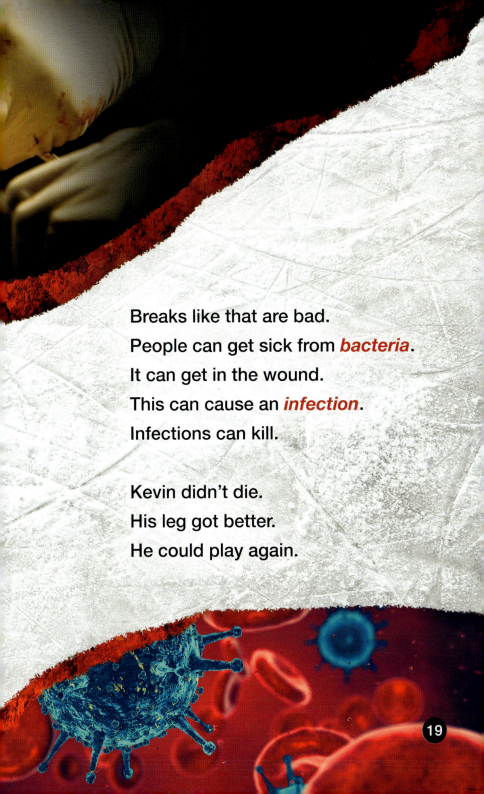

Breaks like that are bad.

People can get sick from *bacteria*.

It can get in the wound.

This can cause an *infection*.

Infections can kill.

Kevin didn't die.

His leg got better.

He could play again.

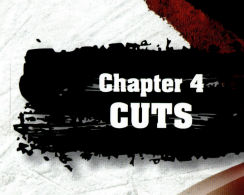

Chapter 4
CUTS

Cuts and scrapes can happen.

Skin isn't thick.

Sharp things go right through it.

Some cuts are small.

Others are deep.

They can be very bloody.

Here's why.

Blood flows through small tubes.

These are called blood *vessels*.

Humans have many miles of blood vessels.

Kids have 60,000 miles.

Adults have 100,000 miles.

YOUR OWN WORST ENEMY

DOYLE ALEXANDER

SPORT: Baseball
INJURY: Broken finger
HOW: Punched a wall with his pitching hand

There are three kinds of blood vessels.

Capillaries are small and thin.

If you cut one, it will bleed.

But it won't bleed much.

Veins are bigger.

They are thicker too.

Veins move blood to the heart.

What if one gets cut?

It will bleed.

There might be a mess.

A bandage may stop the blood.

Stitches may be needed.

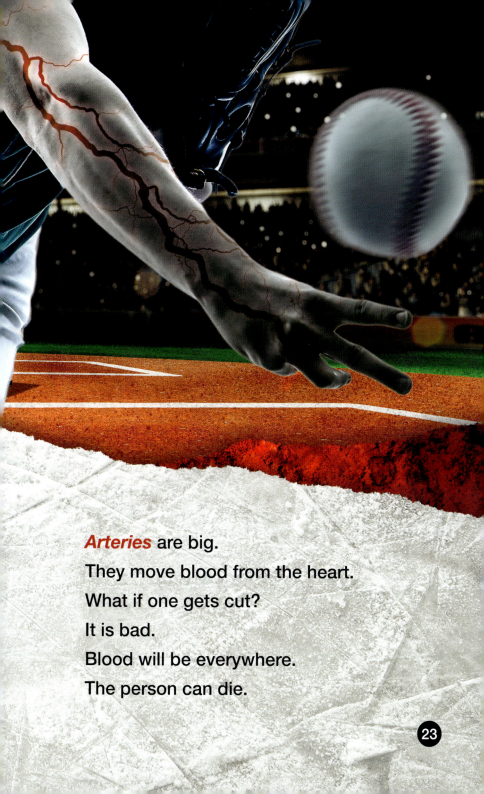

Arteries are big.

They move blood from the heart.

What if one gets cut?

It is bad.

Blood will be everywhere.

The person can die.

It was 1989.

Clint Malarchuk was a hockey player.

He played goalie.

His job was to protect the net.

Two players got near the goal.

They were trying to score.

Crash!

Clint fell.

He pulled off his mask.

His hand went to his neck.

A skate blade had cut it.

The ice turned red.

It was covered with blood.

People watched in horror.

Blood kept coming from his neck.

It didn't stop.

A coach helped.

He pressed hard on the wound.

The blood flow slowed.

Doctors closed the wound.

It took 300 stitches.

Clint lived.

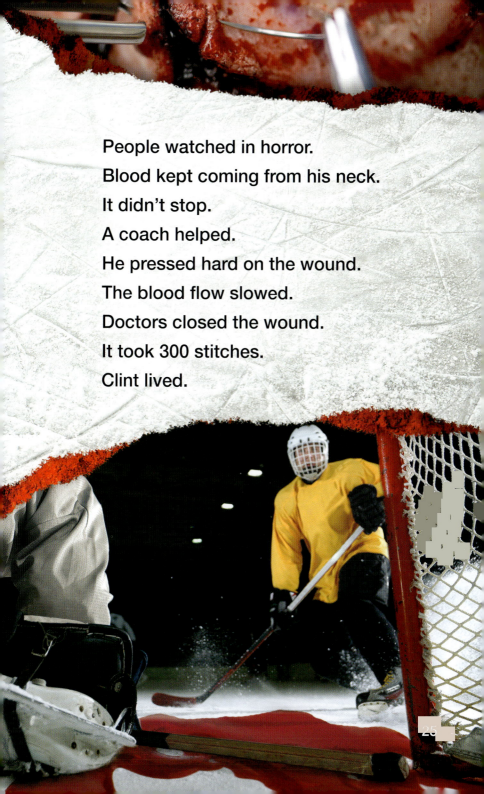

Chapter 5
KNEES

Knees are joints.

They are where leg bones meet.

The upper and lower leg connect.

Ligaments hold bones in place.

They make knees strong.

One is called the *ACL*.

The ACL is thick and stretchy.

It holds the leg bones.

But it's weak.

It can pop, rip, or tear.

It was 2007.

Lindsey Vonn was a skier.

There was a race.

She crashed.

Her knee was hurt.

It made an awful sound.

Pop!

She tore her ACL.
It wasn't too bad.
She rested.
Her knee got better.

Lindsey was in another race in 2013.
Wham!
She crashed again.
This one was bad.
She hurt the same knee.
The ACL tore.
She needed surgery.

LINDSEY VONN

Could it be fixed?

Doctors wanted to try.

They used a *tendon* called the *hamstring*.

It sits behind the knee.

They built a new ACL from it.

Men are lucky.

ACL injuries happen eight times more often to women.

YOUR OWN WORST ENEMY

DAN BOYLE

SPORT: Hockey

INJURY: Sliced tendons

HOW: Skate slipped off hook and blade cut his wrist

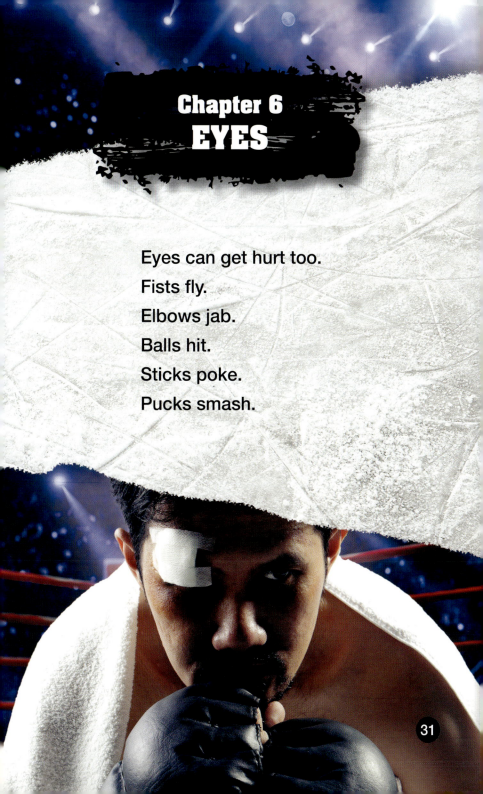

Chapter 6
EYES

Eyes can get hurt too.

Fists fly.

Elbows jab.

Balls hit.

Sticks poke.

Pucks smash.

It was 1979.

Bernie Parent played hockey.

He was a goalie.

His mask was on.

A hockey stick poked him.

It went right through the mask.

His eye was injured.

He couldn't see for weeks.

The *retina* was damaged.

It sits at the back of the eye.

We can't see without it.

Light enters through the *cornea*.

Then it goes through the *pupil* and the *lens*.

At the retina, light sends signals.

Those go to the brain.

The signals tell you what you see.

Bernie recovered.
But he wasn't the same.
He couldn't see very well.
This led him to retire.

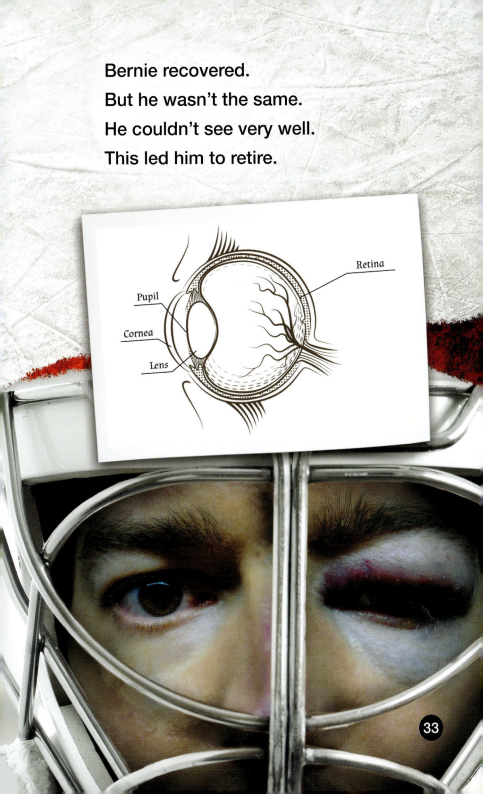

Retina

Pupil

Cornea

Lens

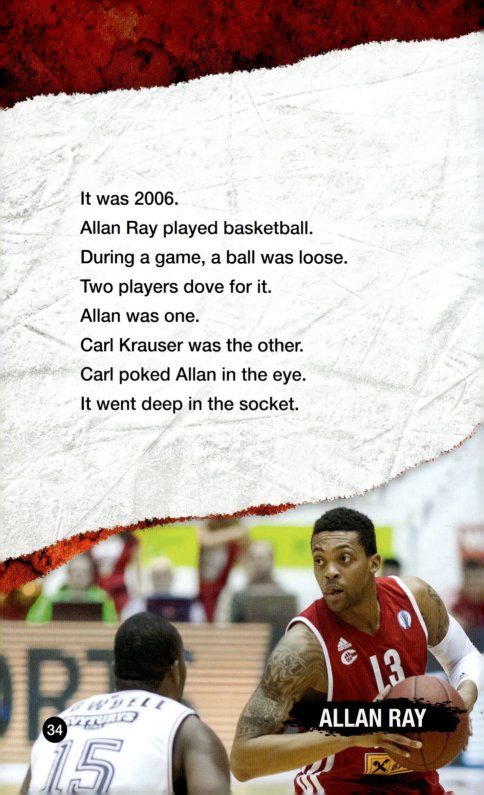

It was 2006.

Allan Ray played basketball.

During a game, a ball was loose.

Two players dove for it.

Allan was one.

Carl Krauser was the other.

Carl poked Allan in the eye.

It went deep in the socket.

ALLAN RAY

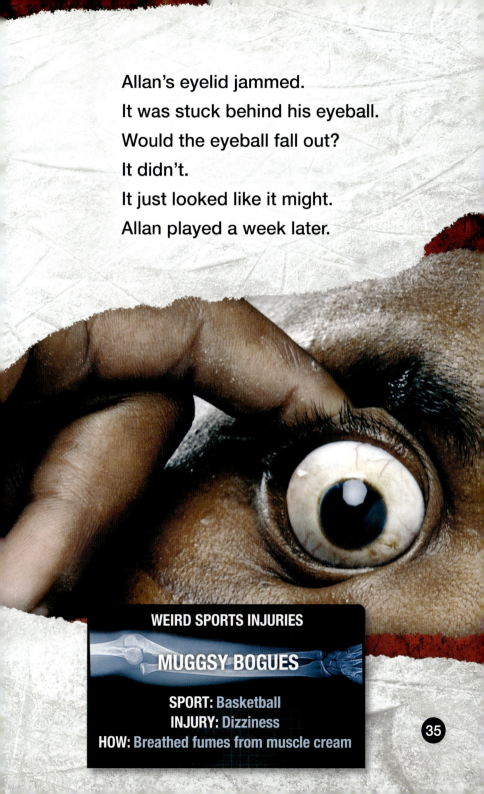

Allan's eyelid jammed.
It was stuck behind his eyeball.
Would the eyeball fall out?
It didn't.
It just looked like it might.
Allan played a week later.

WEIRD SPORTS INJURIES

MUGGSY BOGUES

SPORT: Basketball
INJURY: Dizziness
HOW: Breathed fumes from muscle cream

35

Chapter 7
BODY PARTS

It's hard to lose a body part.

Skin comes apart.

Bones break.

Tendons rip.

Muscles tear.

Nerves split.

Blood vessels shred.

All of this hurts.

It makes a bloody mess.

It was 2013.

Rashad Johnson played football.

The tip of his finger came off.

Rashad didn't even notice.

He kept on playing.

But something felt weird.

He took off his glove.

What did he find?

There was the tip of his middle finger.

The bone was showing.

Doctors could not put the tip back on.

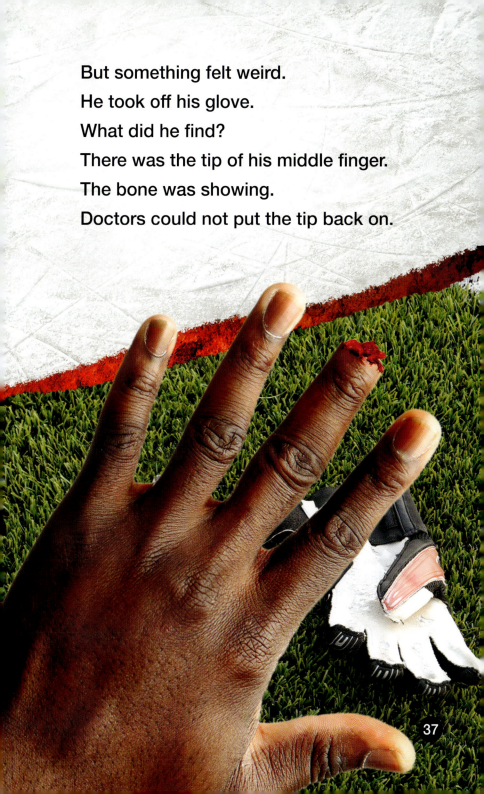

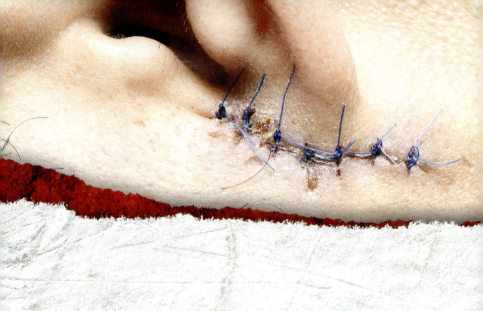

Some athletes have lost an ear.

It happened to Eddie Shore in 1926.

It was a fight with Billy Coutu.

Both played hockey.

Billy grabbed Eddie's ear.

He nearly ripped it off.

The ear hung from Eddie's head.

A doctor stitched it back.

Eddie watched the doctor work in a mirror.

YOUR OWN WORST ENEMY

JOBA CHAMBERLAIN

SPORT: Baseball
INJURY: Hurt ankle
HOW: Fell off a trampoline

39

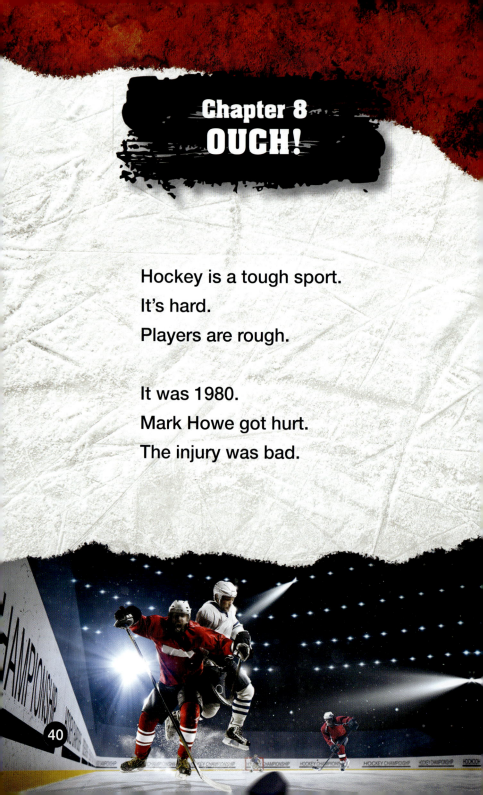

Hockey is a tough sport.

It's hard.

Players are rough.

It was 1980.

Mark Howe got hurt.

The injury was bad.

MARK HOWE

Two players were near the goal.

Mark was there too.

He got bumped.

Mark slid right into the net.

There was a metal part sticking out.

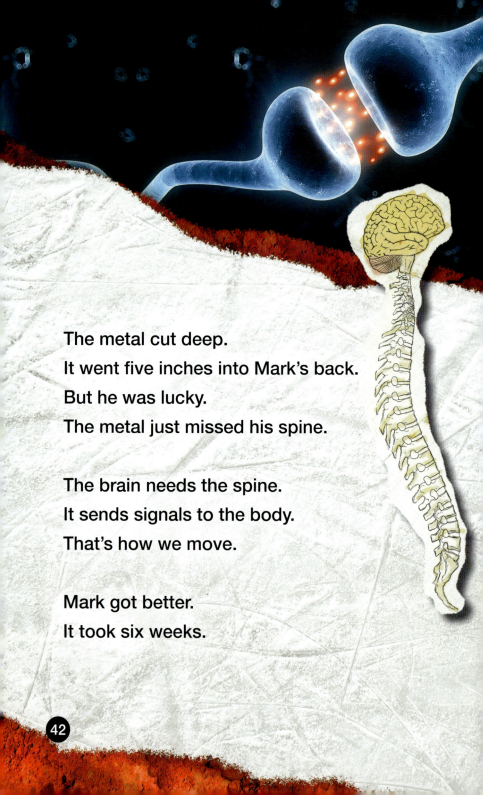

The metal cut deep.

It went five inches into Mark's back.

But he was lucky.

The metal just missed his spine.

The brain needs the spine.

It sends signals to the body.

That's how we move.

Mark got better.

It took six weeks.

Chapter 9
BIG BITES

Babies sometimes bite.

Most adults don't.

But some athletes do.

Ears have tiny bones.

They are the smallest in the body.

The outside of the ear is *cartilage*.

This is tough and flexible.

It gives ears their shape.

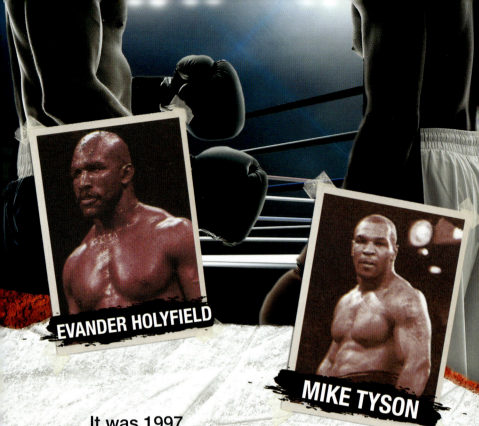

EVANDER HOLYFIELD

MIKE TYSON

It was 1997.

There was a boxing match.

Evander Holyfield and Mike Tyson fought.

Both men were tough.

Mike bit Evander's ear.

He tore a chunk right off.

The fight was stopped.

Mike got kicked out.

What happened to the chunk of ear?

No one knows.

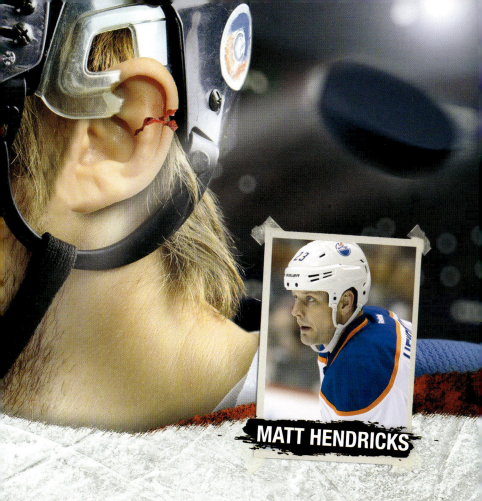

MATT HENDRICKS

Hockey is not good to ears.

It was 2015.

Matt Hendricks split his ear in half.

A puck hit him.

His ear was sewn up.

It didn't slow him down.

He was back on the ice the next day.

Chapter 10
SAFETY

Sports are fun.

But they can be rough.

Legs get broken.

Fingertips get cut off.

Bones poke through skin.

Blood spills.

Knees twist.

It's a high price.

Athletes pay it for many reasons.

Fame, money, or love of the game are just a few.

YOUR OWN WORST ENEMY

GUS FREROTTE

SPORT: Football
INJURY: Hurt his neck
HOW: Rammed his head into a padded
cement wall to celebrate touchdown

Play if you want to.

But do it right.

Be safe.

Wear gear.

Cover with pads.

Put on a helmet.

Wear gloves.

Use a mouth guard.

This will help you avoid injuries.

What if you're in pain?

Don't play.

Rest.

Get well.

Getting hurt isn't worth it.

Injuries are painful.

There can be a lot of blood.

It's gnarly.

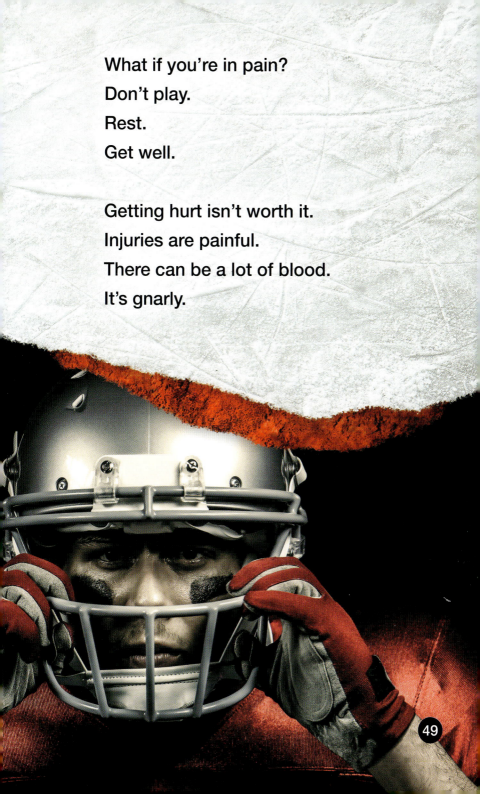

GLOSSARY

ACL: a ligament behind the knee; *anterior cruciate ligament*

artery: a large blood vessel that moves blood away from the heart

bacteria: tiny forms of life that can make a person sick; germs

capillary: the smallest kind of blood vessel

cartilage: tough but flexible tissue found in a person's body

cornea: a clear part in the front of the eye

gnarly: bad or serious; nasty

hamstring: a leg tendon behind the knee

infection: illness caused by bacteria

injury: damage to the body or a part of the body

joint: a part of the body where bones connect, like a knee or elbow

lens: part of the eye that focuses light onto the retina to make an image

ligament: tough tissue that connects bones at a joint

mineral: a chemical important to health, like iron

nerve: a fiber that carries messages to and from the brain

pupil: an opening in the eye where light enters

retina: a layer of cells at the back of the eye that sends signals to the brain

tendon: tough tissue that connects muscle to bone

vein: a blood vessel that carries blood to the heart

vessel: a tube in the body that blood flows through

TAKE A LOOK INSIDE

The SCIENCE of MOVIES

Chapter 6
EXPLOSIONS

Boom!
Fire starts.
There is an explosion.
This happens in some movies.
It looks real.
That's because it is.

Experts plan the blasts.
They may blow up a real building.
Explosives are put on windows.
Glass blows out.
The building falls.
A big fireball brings it down.

They use a fly system.
Long ago it was a big machine.
Wires held an actor.
A worker pulled on a rope.
The actor went up.

Today's system is like that.
But there are fewer parts.

It's not as heavy.
Computers add effects.
They create the setting.
We see blue sky.
Tall buildings rise.
Superman seems to speed by.

Now we have *high-tech* movies.
Color is digital.
There are big special effects.

What's next?
A scientist is out there.
She has a big idea.
Wait and see.
Science will change movies
once again.

red rhino b👓ks®

NONFICTION

9781680210736

9781680210316

9781680210729

9781680210484

9781680210347

9781680210477

9781680210293

9781680210538

9781680210712

9781680210491

9781680210378

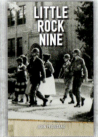

9781680210552

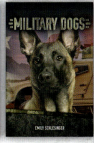

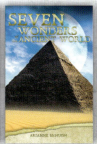